Poetry for Young People

Robert Frost

Edited by Gary D. Schmidt
Illustrated by Henri Sorensen

Sterling Publishing Company, Inc.
New York

For Kenneth W. Kuiper,
who knows that some things gold can stay.

A MAGNOLIA EDITIONS BOOK

Editors: Karla Olson, Loretta Mowat
Art Director/Designer: Jeff Batzli
Production Manager: Jeanne E. Kaufman

Library of Congress Cataloguing in Publication Data
Frost, Robert, 1874-1963.
 Poetry for young people : Robert Frost / edited by Gary D. Schmidt
; illustrated by Henri Sorensen.
  p. cm.
 Includes index
 Summary: A collection of poems about the four seasons by one of
best-known American poets.
 ISBN 0-8069-0633-2
 1. Children's poetry, American. [1. American poetry.]
I. Schmidt, Gary D. II. Sorensen, Henri, ill. III. Title
PS3511.R94A6 1994
811'.52--dc20   94-11161
                                                                                        CIP
                                                                                        AC

8 10 9

Published by Sterling Publishing Company, Inc.
387 Park Avenue South, New York, N.Y. 10016

© 1994 by Magnolia Editions Limited
Illustrations © 1994 Henri Sorensen
Photography p.4: Courtesy of the Jones Library, Inc. Amherst, MA
Distributed in Canada by Sterling Publishing
c/o Canadian Manda Group, One Atlantic Avenue, Suite 105
Toronto, Ontario, Canada M6K 3E7
Distributed in Great Britain and Europe by Cassell PLC
Villiers House, 41/47 Strand, London WC2N 5JE, England
Distributed in Australia by Capricorn Link (Australia) Pty Ltd.
P.O. Box 6651, Baulkham Hills, Business Centre,
NSW 2153, Australia

Printed in China
All rights reserved

Sterling ISBN 0-8069-0633-2

Contents

Robert Frost: A New England Life

IF YOU WALK DOWN A ROAD IN VERMONT IN MID-WINTER, UNDER A bright blue sky with the air so cold it seems to thaw only as you breathe it in, you see mountains piled up against each other, stone fences stretching across fields of dried cornstalks, and white birches with crackling black branches. Your feet crunch against the dry snow, while a crow caws, caws, caws about the cold.

This is the world of Robert Frost's poetry—snow and crows and birches, as well as brooks and asters and hayfields and autumn leaves. Seldom has a poet been so identified with a region as Robert Frost has with New England, though he himself would not have claimed this. His poems have the feel of sudden lines that surprised him. You catch a poem just as it comes, he once said. What he caught were poems about New England—and about life.

On March 26, 1874, Frost was born in San Francisco, which is about as far as you can get from New England and still be in the continental United States. Frost's father was a journalist who edited a city newspaper, and his mother was a teacher. Frost eventually tried his hand at both professions.

His father was born in the South but moved to New Hampshire to become a journalist. He left the region during the Civil War (perhaps because he did not want to be seen as a Yankee) and moved to California. As if to tweak the nose of New England, he named his son after the South's most famous general, Robert E. Lee. But after his father's death in 1885, eleven-year-old Robert, his sister Jeanie, and their mother returned to New England. The family had no money, so they lived with Robert's grandfather in Lawrence, Massachussetts.

It is never easy to return home, though. Frost hated his work as a bobbin boy in his grandfather's mills. He disliked his grandfather's strictness and the way he made Frost's mother feel responsible for his father's death. Soon his mother could stand it no longer. She went a few miles south to Salem, New Hampshire, to teach, settling herself and her family with a nearby farmwife. The pay was poor, so Frost took a job as a cobbler, nailing heels to boots, to help pay the rent.

Frost did well at the village school in Salem. During the next three years, Frost's grandfather offered to pay for the train fare that would allow him to attend Lawrence High School. Frost was elated and soon became the top student in his class.

When Frost was sixteen, he began to write poetry, jotting down words that seemed to just come into his mind. But he was not yet thinking of becoming a poet. Perhaps he was thinking more about Elinor White, with whom he had shared the highest honors in his school when they graduated in 1892.

The years after his graduation were frustrating for Frost. His grandfather demanded that he go on to Dartmouth, but Frost wasn't interested in college. He was interested in poetry, however, and soon all he was doing was wandering through the woods reading a collection of British poems, so he left Dartmouth and returned to Lawrence. He worked in the mills again and kept reading and writing. When he was nineteen, he sent his first poem to a magazine called *The Independent*. It was accepted, and Robert Frost knew he wanted to be a poet.

Even a poet needs income, so he tried his father's profession—writing for a weekly newspaper called *The Sentinel*. He liked the writing, but hated prying into things he thought were none of his business. He quit after only a few months, then taught school with his mother and sister. In 1895, Elinor White came to teach with them, and soon afterward, in December, she and Frost were married. But Frost did not enjoy teaching young children, and there was little money coming in.

The following year, the Frosts had a son. To earn more money the new father decided that he would be a college teacher, but first he had to finish college himself. With help from his grandfather, he began studies at New England's most prestigious university, Harvard, but the courses bored him. He became sick; but even worse, his son Eliot also grew ill, and then died.

There seemed no reason to stay at Harvard. Frost left without finishing, which meant he could not teach college. Elinor begged Frost's grandfather to help them buy a farm.

Grandfather was reluctant, but willing. If Frost would commit himself to working the farm for ten years, his grandfather would pay for it. Frost agreed, and in 1900, he, Elinor, and their new baby daughter settled into a dairy farm in Derry, New Hampshire. During the day, he did all the chores to keep the farm going; at night, when the house was completely still, he wrote poetry. Those were the years when he wrote such poems as "Mending Wall" and "October."

It was hard for Frost to make a go of his rocky farm, especially since he had three more children over the next five years. Money was scarce, but when the director of the Pinkerton Academy heard Frost read one of his poems, he was impressed. He asked Frost to teach an English class two days each week, and Frost agreed. He needed the money for food.

Frost stayed for the ten years he promised his grandfather, and then sold the farm. He had never liked the busy schedule of a farmer, and he suffered from hay fever, so he couldn't cut his own hay. Although editors rejected his poems over the years because they seemed too modern, Frost knew he had to keep trying. The family had to find a place where they could live on little money and where Frost would be free to write his poetry. Perhaps thinking of the British poets he had read at Dartmouth, Frost decided to go to England.

In the autumn of 1912, Frost and his family settled into a small country farmhouse thatched with thick straw. Ignoring the pile of rejection letters that he had received from editors in the U.S., Frost brought thirty of his poems to a publisher in London. Three days later, he heard that they had been accepted for a book. Within a year, this New England poet's life as a professional began: *A Boy's Will* was published in 1913, followed by *North of Boston* the next year. When the books were reprinted in America, Frost said to Elinor, "My book has gone home; we must go too," and so the Frost family returned to New England in 1914.

Frost came back to a country with arms open wide to receive him. Editors who had earlier rejected his poems were anxious to publish them. But his poetry was still not making much money, and his first two books earned him only two hundred dollars.

As the family settled in, Frost looked about his world for inspiration. He saw birches and fields and mountains, and those are what he wrote about. He walked across upland pastures and wrote "The Vantage Point." He explored a forest whose leaves had turned golden in the autumn chill and wrote "The Road Not Taken." He watched cows munching on apples and wrote "The Cow in Apple Time." He saw boys climbing birch trees and wrote "Birches."

The years after his return from England were busy. His poems were praised by critics, and people came to New England to meet him. They also asked him to read at colleges such as Amherst, Harvard, Yale, Dartmouth, and Michigan. The trips interrupted his writing, and he always seemed to come back with a cold, but he went, because the reading brought in money.

As he became better known, Frost was asked to teach—first at Amherst, then at other universities—and his dream of becoming a college teacher finally came true. In fact, in 1920 he even helped to start a college—the Bread Loaf School of English in Vermont. He was a challenging, witty, and sometimes grouchy teacher, once throwing away a whole pile of compositions his students had written. But his students loved him, for he made them think.

In 1923 Frost published *New Hampshire*, which won the Pulitzer Prize, one of the country's most prestigious awards. Seven years later, he won his second Pulitzer for his *Collected Poems*, and then, astonishingly, a third Pulitzer in 1936 for *A Further Range*. No one was surprised when he won his fourth Pulitzer Prize in 1942. These books, together with his teaching and many speaking tours, finally earned him the money that had previously eluded him.

In 1957, Frost attended a dinner in England held in his honor. T.S. Eliot, the greatest English poet then living, gave the toast. He also had lived in New England, and he knew what Frost was writing about. Frost, he said, was writing about the whole world, about feelings and ideas that everyone, everywhere, understood. Those who were there saw that Frost nearly began to weep.

The next year, Frost spoke at Bread Loaf, thinking of that toast by T.S. Eliot. "There ought to be in everything you write some sign that you come from almost anywhere," he said. Perhaps that is what keeps Robert Frost so alive today, even to people who have never set foot in Vermont. In writing about New England, Frost was also writing about everywhere.

Frost became the country's most beloved poet. He received the formal congratulations of the United States Senate when he turned seventy-five, and again a decade later. The next year, he read his poem "The Gift Outright" at the inauguration of President John F. Kennedy. When he died three years later, people around the world mourned, many remembering him for what he was—a great poet.

Poems of Summer

THE PASTURE

I'm going out to clean the pasture spring;
I'll only stop to rake the leaves away
(And wait to watch the water clear, I may)
I sha'n't be gone long.—You come too.

I'm going out to fetch the little calf
That's standing by the mother. It's so young
It totters when she licks it with her tongue.
I sha'n't be gone long.—You come too.

Robert Frost used "The Pasture" to introduce his poetry. In this poem, he seems to be talking perhaps to a friend, someone he loves, or a stranger who has stopped by. He asks the listener to come out to the pasture with him, to see the things that he will see. But Frost is also asking his reader to come into his world—a world of pastures, leaves, springs, and young calves newly born.

ROSE POGONIAS

A saturated meadow,
  Sun-shaped and jewel-small,
A circle scarcely wider
  Than the trees around were tall;
Where winds were quite excluded,
  And the air was stifling sweet
With the breath of many flowers,—
  A temple of the heat.

There we bowed us in the burning,
  As the sun's right worship is,
To pick where none could miss them
  A thousand orchises;
For though the grass was scattered,
  Yet every second spear
Seemed tipped with wings of color,
  That tinged the atmosphere.

We raised a simple prayer
  Before we left the spot,
That in the general mowing
  That place might be forgot;
Or if not all so favored,
  Obtain such grace of hours,
That none should mow the grass there
  While so confused with flowers.

Flowers last only a short time, especially if they are growing in a hayfield, where they will be cut and harvested along with the hay. But Frost, thinking about how short and sweet beauty is, tries in this poem to find a way to keep the flowers—and their beauty— from being cut.

THE TUFT OF FLOWERS

I went to turn the grass once after one
Who mowed it in the dew before the sun.

The dew was gone that made his blade so keen
Before I came to view the leveled scene.

I looked for him behind an isle of trees;
I listened for his whetstone on the breeze.

But he had gone his way, the grass all mown,
And I must be, as he had been,—alone,

"As all must be," I said within my heart,
"Whether they work together or apart."

But as I said it, swift there passed me by
On noiseless wing a bewildered butterfly,

Seeking with memories grown dim o'er night
Some resting flower of yesterday's delight.

And once I marked his flight go round and round,
As where some flower lay withering on the ground.

And then he flew as far as eye could see,
And then on tremulous wing came back to me.

I thought of questions that have no reply,
And would have turned to toss the grass to dry;

But he turned first, and led my eye to look
At a tall tuft of flowers beside a brook,

A leaping tongue of bloom the scythe had spared
Beside a reedy brook the scythe had bared.

The mower in the dew had loved them thus,
By leaving them to flourish, not for us,

Nor yet to draw one thought of ours to him,
But from sheer morning gladness at the brim.

The butterfly and I had lit upon,
Nevertheless, a message from the dawn,

That made me hear the wakening birds around,
And hear his long scythe whispering to the ground,

And feel a spirit kindred to my own;
So that henceforth I worked no more alone;

But glad with him, I worked as with his aid,
And weary, sought at noon with him the shade;

And dreaming, as it were, held brotherly speech
With one whose thought I had not hoped to reach.

"Men work together," I told him from the heart,
"Whether they work together or apart."

After a hayfield has been mown, the long grass has to be turned over after a time so that it will dry on both sides and not rot. This can be a boring job, especially if you are doing it alone and by hand. That's how this poem begins—with a man working alone and facing a dull day—but not how it ends. Written in couplets (pairs of rhyming lines), the poem seems to mirror the rhythm of a scythe.

11

AN ENCOUNTER

Once on the kind of day called "weather breeder,"
When the heat slowly hazes and the sun
By its own power seems to be undone,
I was half boring through, half climbing through
A swamp of cedar. Choked with oil of cedar
And scurf of plants, and weary and over-heated,
And sorry I ever left the road I knew,
I paused and rested on a sort of hook
That had me by the coat as good as seated,
And since there was no other way to look,
Looked up toward heaven, and there against the blue,
Stood over me a resurrected tree,
A tree that had been down and raised again—
A barkless specter. He had halted too,
As if for fear of treading upon me.
I saw the strange position of his hands—
Up at his shoulders, dragging yellow strands
Of wire with something in it from men to men.
"You here?" I said. "Where aren't you nowadays?
And what's the news you carry—if you know?
And tell me where you're off for—Montreal?
Me? I'm not off for anywhere at all.
Sometimes I wander out of beaten ways
Half looking for the orchid Calypso."

At times in his poetry, Frost brings together two images that
you would never expect to see together. In this poem, he is
out for a walk in the woods and comes upon "a barkless
specter." Watch for the clues that Frost gives as to what this
specter might be, and why it is so unusual to come upon it in
the middle of the woods.

GHOST HOUSE

I dwell in a lonely house I know
That vanished many a summer ago,
  And left no trace but the cellar walls,
  And a cellar in which the daylight falls,
And the purple-stemmed wild raspberries grow.

O'er ruined fences the grapevines shield
The woods come back to the mowing field;
  The orchard tree has grown one copse
  Of new wood and old where the woodpecker
    chops;
The footpath down to the well is healed.

I dwell with a strangely aching heart
In that vanished abode there far apart
  On that disused and forgotten road
  That has no dust-bath now for the toad.
Night comes; the black bats tumble and dart;

The whippoorwill is coming to shout
And hush and cluck and flutter about:
  I hear him begin far enough away
  Full many a time to say his say
Before he arrives to say it out.

It is under the small, dim, summer star.
I know not who these mute folks are
  Who share the unlit place with me—
  Those stones out under the low-limbed tree
Doubtless bear names that the mosses mar.

They are tireless folk, but slow and sad,
Though two, close-keeping, are lass and lad,—
  With none among them that ever sings,
  And yet, in view of how many things,
As sweet companions as might be had.

The house in this poem has been long abandoned; nothing is left of it but the cellar walls. It was probably once a farmhouse, since the raspberries, grapevines, and mowing field all suggest that the land around it was once farmed. As a child plays in the forgotten rooms, he imagines those who once lived there.

A Girl's Garden

A neighbor of mine in the village
  Likes to tell how one spring
When she was a girl on the farm, she did
  A childlike thing.

One day she asked her father
  To give her a garden plot
To plant and tend and reap herself,
  And he said, "Why not?"

In casting about for a corner
  He thought of an idle bit
Of walled-off ground where a shop had stood,
  And he said, "Just it."

And he said, "That ought to make you
  An ideal one-girl farm,
And give you a chance to put some strength
  On your slim-jim arm."

It was not enough of a garden,
  Her father said, to plow;
So she had to work it all by hand,
  But she don't mind now.

She wheeled the dung in the wheelbarrow
  Along a stretch of road;
But she always ran away and left
  Her not-nice load,

And hid from anyone passing.
  And then she begged the seed.
She says she thinks she planted one
  Of all things but weed.

A hill each of potatoes,
  Radishes, lettuce, peas,
Tomatoes, beets, beans, pumpkins, corn
  And even fruit trees.

And yes, she has long mistrusted
  That a cider apple tree
In bearing there today is hers,
  Or at least may be.

Her crop was a miscellany
  When all was said and done,
A little bit of everything,
  A great deal of none.

Now when she sees in the village
  How village things go,
Just when it seems to come in right,
  She says, "*I* know!

"It's as when I was a farmer—"
  Oh, never by way of advice!
And she never sins by telling the tale
  To the same person twice.

This poem about a young girl's garden is meant to be humorous, so Frost gives it a light and bouncing rhythm. But even though the story is a funny one, Frost makes a serious point about human nature.

THE VANTAGE POINT

If tired of trees I seek again mankind,
  Well I know where to hie me—in the dawn,
  To a slope where the cattle keep the lawn.
There amid lolling juniper reclined,
Myself unseen, I see in white defined
  Far off the homes of men, and farther still,
  The graves of men on an opposing hill,
Living or dead, whichever are to mind.

And if by noon I have too much of these,
  I have but to turn on my arm, and lo,
  The sunburned hillside sets my face aglow,
My breathing shakes the bluet like a breeze,
  I smell the earth, I smell the bruisèd plant.
  I look into the crater of the ant.

A vantage point is a place that allows you to see all around you. In this poem Frost looks at two different worlds—nature and humanity—and seems at home in both.

HYLA BROOK

By June our brook's run out of song and speed.
Sought for much after that, it will be found
Either to have gone groping underground
(And taken with it all the Hyla breed
That shouted in the mist a month ago,
Like ghost of sleigh bells in a ghost of snow)—
Or flourished and come up in jewel-weed,
Weak foliage that is blown upon and bent,
Even against the way its waters went.
Its bed is left a faded paper sheet
Of dead leaves stuck together by the heat—
A brook to none but who remember long.
This as it will be seen is other far
Than with brooks taken otherwhere in song.
We love the things we love for what they are.

Many poems are written to celebrate beautiful rivers and pleasant streams, but this one is about a brook that can run dry. Still, for the poet there seems to be something quite special about it.

Poems of
Autumn

THE LAST WORD
OF A BLUEBIRD

As told to a child

As I went out a Crow
In a low voice said, "Oh,
I was looking for you.
How do you do?
I just came to tell you
To tell Lesley (will you?)
That her little Bluebird
Wanted me to bring word
That the north wind last night
That made the stars bright
And made ice on the trough

Almost made him cough
His tail feathers off.
He just had to fly!
But he sent her Good-by,
And said to be good,
And wear her red hood,
And look for skunk tracks
In the snow with an ax—
And do everything!
And perhaps in the spring
He would come back and sing."

In this poem, a crow speaks, bringing the message of a bluebird who is flying south for the winter.

The Road Not Taken

Two roads diverged in a yellow wood,
And sorry I could not travel both
And be one traveler, long I stood
And looked down one as far as I could
To where it bent in the undergrowth;

Then took the other, as just as fair,
And having perhaps the better claim,
Because it was grassy and wanted wear;
Though as for that the passing there
Had worn them really about the same,

And both that morning equally lay
In leaves no step had trodden black.
Oh, I kept the first for another day!
Yet knowing how way leads on to way,
I doubted if I should ever come back.

I shall be telling this with a sigh
Somewhere ages and ages hence:
Two roads diverged in a wood, and I—
I took the one less traveled by,
And that has made all the difference.

We all know the feel of a cool autumn day, when we can shuffle our feet through fallen leaves and kick up the smells of the season. This is a poem about such a walk, about coming to a fork in the path, and about making choices in our lives.

In Hardwood Groves

The same leaves over and over again!
They fall from giving shade above
To make one texture of faded brown
And fit the earth like a leather glove.

Before the leaves can mount again
To fill the trees with another shade,
They must go down past things coming up.
They must go down into the dark decayed.

They *must* be pierced by flowers and put
Beneath the feet of dancing flowers.
However it is in some other world
I know that this is the way in ours.

*Walking through a grove of hardwood trees—perhaps maples or oaks—
Frost recognizes that before things are raised up, they must fall down. He uses
some startling images, such as flowers piercing dead leaves, and a simile, in
which he compares the leaves to a leather glove.*

OCTOBER

O hushed October morning mild,
Thy leaves have ripened to the fall;
Tomorrow's wind, if it be wild,
Should waste them all.
The crows above the forest call;
Tomorrow they may form and go.
O hushed October morning mild,
Begin the hours of this day slow.
Make the day seem to us less brief.
Hearts not averse to being beguiled,
Beguile us in the way you know.
Release one leaf at break of day;
At noon release another leaf;
One from our trees, one far away.
Retard the sun with gentle mist;
Enchant the land with amethyst.
Slow, slow!
For the grapes' sake, if they were all,
Whose leaves already are burnt with frost,
Whose clustered fruit must else be lost—
For the grapes' sake along the wall.

*A New England October can have days that seem
like winter. In this poem, Frost wants to put off those
wintry days and keep the golden fullness of autumn.
He speaks directly to October, in a kind of prayer.*

THE COW IN APPLE TIME

Something inspires the only cow of late
To make no more of a wall than an open gate,
And think no more of wall-builders than fools.
Her face is flecked with pomace and she drools
A cider syrup. Having tasted fruit,
She scorns a pasture withering to the root.
She runs from tree to tree where lie and sweeten
The windfalls spiked with stubble and worm-eaten.
She leaves them bitten when she has to fly.
She bellows on a knoll against the sky.
Her udder shrivels and the milk goes dry.

In this poem a cow has left the dry grass of its pasture and has started to eat fallen apples. Frost uses couplets—pairs of rhyming lines—to give the poem a light and pleasing rhythm. But something happens and Frost points it out by changing from couplets to three lines rhyming together.

A LATE WALK

When I go up through the mowing field,
  The headless aftermath,
Smooth-laid like thatch with the heavy dew,
  Half closes the garden path.

And when I come to the garden ground,
  The whir of sober birds
Up from the tangle of withered weeds
  Is sadder than any words.

A tree beside the wall stands bare,
  But a leaf that lingered brown,
Disturbed, I doubt not, by my thought,
  Comes softly rattling down.

I end not far from my going forth,
  By picking the faded blue
Of the last remaining aster flower
  To carry again to you.

In late autumn, you can sometimes walk through a field and see things that remind you of summer. Here, Frost finds one last flower, an aster, and brings it back as a reminder.

AFTER APPLE-PICKING

My long two-pointed ladder's sticking through a tree
Toward heaven still,
And there's a barrel that I didn't fill
Beside it, and there may be two or three
Apples I didn't pick upon some bough.
But I am done with apple-picking now.
Essence of winter sleep is on the night,
The scent of apples: I am drowsing off.
I cannot rub the strangeness from my sight
I got from looking through a pane of glass
I skimmed this morning from the drinking trough
And held against the world of hoary grass.
It melted, and I let it fall and break.

But I was well
Upon my way to sleep before it fell,
And I could tell
What form my dreaming was about to take.
Magnified apples appear and disappear,
Stem end and blossom end,
And every fleck of russet showing clear.
My instep arch not only keeps the ache,
It keeps the pressure of a ladder-round.
I feel the ladder sway as the boughs bend.
And I keep hearing from the cellar bin
The rumbling sound
Of load on load of apples coming in.
For I have had too much
Of apple-picking: I am overtired
Of the great harvest I myself desired.
There were ten thousand thousand fruit to touch,
Cherish in hand, lift down, and not let fall.
For all
That struck the earth,
No matter if not bruised or spiked with stubble,
Went surely to the cider-apple heap
As of no worth.
One can see what will trouble
This sleep of mine, whatever sleep it is.
Were he not gone,
The woodchuck could say whether its like his
Long sleep, as I describe its coming on,
Or just some human sleep.

Apple-picking can be slow work. Each apple must be picked by hand, while you hold yourself secure on the ladder with your legs. Any apple that falls or is dropped will bruise and then rot, spoiling any other apples that are stored with it. In this poem, the weather is starting to turn wintry—there is already ice on the water trough—and Frost is looking forward to a long winter's sleep.

GOING FOR WATER

The well was dry beside the door,
  And so we went with pail and can
Across the fields behind the house
  To seek the brook if still it ran;

Not loth to have excuse to go,
  Because the autumn eve was fair
(Though chill), because the fields were ours,
  And by the brook our woods were there.

We ran as if to meet the moon
  That slowly danced behind the trees,
The barren boughs without the leaves,
  Without the birds, without the breeze.

But once within the wood, we paused
  Like gnomes that hid us from the moon,
Ready to run to hiding new,
  With laughter when she found us soon.

Each laid on other a staying hand
  To listen ere we dared to look,
And in the hush we joined to make
  We heard, we knew we heard the brook

A note as from a single place,
  A slender tinkling fall that made
Now drops that floated on the pool
  Like pearls, and now a silver blade.

It is late autumn in this poem, and the brooks are starting to freeze up. But late at night, two people watch the moon rise and go toward the brook, and they know by its sound that the brook is still open.

OUT, OUT—

The buzz saw snarled and rattled in the yard
And made dust and dropped stove-length sticks of wood,
Sweet-scented stuff when the breeze drew across it.
And from there those that lifted eyes could count
Five mountain ranges one behind the other
Under the sunset far into Vermont.
And the saw snarled and rattled, snarled and rattled,
As it ran light, or had to bear a load.
And nothing happened: day was all but done.
Call it a day, I wish they might have said
To please the boy by giving him the half hour
That a boy counts so much when saved from work.
His sister stood beside them in her apron
To tell them "Supper." At the word, the saw,
As if to prove saws knew what supper meant,
Leaped out at the boy's hand, or seemed to leap—
He must have given the hand. However it was,
Neither refused the meeting. But the hand!
The boy's first outcry was a rueful laugh,
As he swung toward them holding up the hand
Half in appeal, but half as if to keep
The life from spilling. Then the boy saw all—
Since he was old enough to know, big boy
Doing a man's work, though a child at heart—
He saw all spoiled. "Don't let them cut my hand off—
The doctor, when he comes. Don't let him, sister!"
So. But the hand was gone already.
The doctor put him in the dark of ether.
He lay and puffed his lips out with his breath.
And then—the watcher at his pulse took fright.
No one believed. They listened at his heart.
Little—less—nothing!—and that ended it.
No more to build on there. And they, since they
Were not the one dead, turned to their affairs.

This is a story about a boy cutting wood to use for winter fires. The scene starts calm and peaceful, but there is a dreadful accident. The last line of the poem is painful. Is the speaker saying that these people were heartless? Or is he saying that life must always go on, even in the face of death?

Poems of
Winter

NOW CLOSE THE WINDOWS

Now close the windows and hush all the fields:
  If the trees must, let them silently toss;
No bird is singing now, and if there is,
  Be it my loss.

It will be long ere the marshes resume,
  It will be long ere the earliest bird:
So close the windows and not hear the wind,
  But see all wind-stirred.

When winter comes in New England, houses need to be shut against the cold. This is a poem about closing the windows, but it is also about being comfortable at home, looking out from a warm room to the cold outside.

WIND AND WINDOW FLOWER

Lovers, forget your love,
  And list to the love of these.
She a window flower,
  And he a winter breeze.

When the frosty window veil
  Was melted down at noon,
And the caged yellow bird
  Hung over her in tune,

He marked her through the pane
  He could not help but mark,
And only passed her by,
  To come again at dark.

He was a winter wind,
  Concerned with ice and snow,
Dead weeds and unmated birds,
  And little of love could know.

But he sighed upon the sill,
  He gave the sash a shake,
As witness all within
  Who lay that night awake.

Perchance he half prevailed
  To win her for the flight
From the firelit looking-glass
  And warm stove-window light.

But the flower leaned aside
  And thought of naught to say,
And morning found the breeze
  A hundred miles away.

It is hard to imagine a winter wind loving a window flower, especially when the flower is set against the window as a reminder that spring will come. Perhaps this is what the wind comes to realize as well, because the flower is not interested in him.

A PATCH OF OLD SNOW

There's a patch of old snow in a corner
  That I should have guessed
Was a blow-away paper the rain
  Had brought to rest.

It is speckled with grime as if
  Small print overspread it,
The news of a day I've forgotten—
  If I ever read it.

Toward the end of winter, when most of the snow has melted, Frost finds a small patch of dirty snow, perhaps shaded from the sun. Watch how this single image makes him think about the past.

GOOD HOURS

I had for my winter evening walk—
No one at all with whom to talk,
But I had the cottages in a row
Up to their shining eyes in snow.

And I thought I had the folk within:
I had the sound of a violin;
I had a glimpse through curtain laces
Of youthful forms and youthful faces.

I had such company outward bound.
I went till there were no cottages found.
I turned and repented, but coming back
I saw no window but that was black.

Over the snow my creaking feet
Disturbed the slumbering village street
Like profanation, by your leave,
At ten o'clock of a winter eve.

In many of Frost's poems he walks along a path and comments on what he sees. Here, on a cold winter's night, he feels the companionship of those inside the houses he passes.

THE WOOD-PILE

Out walking in the frozen swamp one gray day,
I paused and said, "I will turn back from here.
No, I will go on farther—and we shall see."
The hard snow held me, save where now and then
One foot went through. The view was all in lines
Straight up and down of tall slim trees
Too much alike to mark or name a place by
So as to say for certain I was here
Or somewhere else: I was just far from home.
A small bird flew before me. He was careful
To put a tree between us when he lighted,
And say no word to tell me who he was
Who was so foolish as to think what *he* thought.
He thought that I was after him for a feather—
The white one in his tail; like one who takes
Everything said as personal to himself.
One flight out sideways would have undeceived him.
And then there was a pile of wood for which
I forgot him and let his little fear
Carry him off the way I might have gone,
WIthout so much as wishing him good-night.
He went behind it to make his last stand.
It was a cord of maple, cut and split
And piled—and measured, four by four by eight.
And not another like it could I see.
No runner tracks in this year's snow looped near it.

And it was older sure than this year's cutting,
Or even last year's or the year's before.
The wood was gray and the bark warping off it
And the pile somewhat sunken. Clematis
Had wound strings round and round it like a bundle.
What held it though on one side was a tree
Still growing, and on one a stake and prop,
These latter about to fall. I thought that only
Someone who lived in turning to fresh tasks
Could so forget his handiwork on which
He spent himself, the labor of his ax,
And leave it there far from a useful fireplace
To warm the frozen swamp as best it could
With the slow smokeless burning of decay.

In New England, wood for winter is cut the previous winter so that it can be slid on snow out of the woods. Here, a neatly stacked wood-pile seems ready to be taken out, but it has stood there for some time, rotting in the snow. The image makes Frost think about what might have happened.

STORM FEAR

When the wind works against us in the dark,
And pelts with snow
The lower chamber window on the east,
And whispers with a sort of stifled bark,
The beast,
"Come out! Come out!"—
It costs no inward struggle not to go,
Ah, no!

I count our strength,
Two and a child,
Those of us not asleep subdued to mark
How the cold creeps as the fire dies at length—
How drifts are piled,
Dooryard and road ungraded,
Till even the comforting barn grows far away,
And my heart owns a doubt
Whether 'tis in us to arise with day
And save ourselves unaided.

As in "Now Close the Windows" (page 32), Frost thinks about his family watching the winter from their warm house, but this time there is a fearful snowstorm.

Poems of
Spring

A PRAYER IN SPRING

Oh, give us pleasure in the flowers today;
And give us not to think so far away
As the uncertain harvest; keep us here
All simply in the springing of the year.

Oh, give us pleasure in the orchard white,
Like nothing else by day, like ghosts by night;
And make us happy in the happy bees,
The swarm dilating round the perfect trees.

And make us happy in the darting bird
That suddenly above the bees is heard,
The meteor that thrusts in with needle bill,
And off a blossom in mid air stands still.

For this is love and nothing else is love,
The which it is reserved for God above
To sanctify to what far ends He will,
But which it only needs that we fulfill.

Frost often wrote about time, about how things change and cannot stay the way they are. In this poem he looks around him and sees the glorious beauty of a spring day, and he prays that it could somehow be kept so that it would not disappear. In fact, the poet sees the day as being love itself, something that is sanctified; but even as he utters the prayer, he knows that it cannot be answered.

A TIME TO TALK

When a friend calls to me from the road
And slows his horse to a meaning walk,
I don't stand still and look around
On all the hills I haven't hoed,
And shout from where I am, "What is it?"
No, not as there is a time to talk.
I thrust my hoe in the mellow ground,
Blade-end up and five feet tall,
And plod: I go up to the stone wall
For a friendly visit.

A gardener in the middle of his work may not always want to stop his summertime hoeing, but in this poem the gardener pauses for a friend. He is quite different from the neighbor in "Mending Wall" (page 46), who will not interrupt his work for a friendly chat. The last line is short, as though he is stopping the poem so he can go for his visit.

TO THE THAWING WIND

Come with rain, O loud Southwester!
Bring the singer, bring the nester;
Give the buried flower a dream;
Make the settled snowbank steam;
Find the brown beneath the white;
But whate'er you do tonight,
Bathe my window, make it flow,
Melt it as the ice will go;

Melt the glass and leave the sticks
Like a hermit's crucifix;
Burst into my narrow stall;
Swing the picture on the wall;
Run the rattling pages o'er;
Scatter poems on the floor;
Turn the poet out of door.

First the poem calls to the thawing wind, asking it to bring an end to winter and to usher in spring. But soon it changes, as we learn that the speaker is also a poet. By the end he is asking the wind to bring him inspiration for his poetry, to bring him and it new life outdoors.

PEA BRUSH

I walked down alone Sunday after church
  To the place where John has been cutting trees,
To see for myself about the birch
  He said I could have to brush my peas.

The sun in the new-cut narrow gap
  Was hot enough for the first of May,
And stifling hot with the odor of sap
  From stumps still bleeding their life away.

The frogs that were peeping a thousand shrill
  Wherever the ground was low and wet,
The minute they heard my step went still
  To watch me and see what I came to get.

Birch boughs enough piled everywhere!—
  All fresh and sound from the recent ax.
Time someone came with cart and pair
  And got them off the wild flowers' backs.

They might be good for garden things
  To curl a little finger round,
The same as you seize cat's-cradle strings
  And lift themselves up off the ground.

Small good to anything growing wild,
  They were crooking many a trillium
That had budded before the boughs were piled
  And since it was coming up had to come.

Birch boughs can be good for staking up peas, because peas send little tendrils like fingers to climb up stakes. But when Frost finds some birch boughs in this poem, they are doing something quite different.

BIRCHES

When I see birches bend to left and right
Across the lines of straighter darker trees,
I like to think some boy's been swinging them.
But swinging doesn't bend them down to stay
As ice storms do. Often you must have seen them
Loaded with ice a sunny winter morning
After a rain. They click upon themselves
As the breeze rises, and turn many-colored
As the stir cracks and crazes their enamel.
Soon the sun's warmth makes them shed crystal shells
Shattering and avalanching on the snow-crust—
Such heaps of broken glass to sweep away
You'd think the inner dome of heaven had fallen.
They are dragged to the withered bracken by the load,
And they seem not to break; though once they are bowed
So low for long, they never right themselves:
You may see their trunks arching in the woods
Years afterwards, trailing their leaves on the ground
Like girls on hands and knees that throw their hair
Before them over their heads to dry in the sun.
But I was going to say when Truth broke in
With all her matter of fact about the ice-storm
I should prefer to have some boy bend them
As he went out and in to fetch the cows—
Some boy too far from town to learn baseball,
Whose only play was what he found himself,
Summer or winter, and could play alone.
One by one he subdued his father's trees
By riding them down over and over again
Until he took the stiffness out of them,
And not one but hung limp, not one was left
For him to conquer. He learned all there was
To learn about not launching out too soon
And so not carrying the tree away
Clear to the ground. He always kept his poise
To the top branches, climbing carefully
With the same pains you use to fill a cup
Up to the brim, and even above the brim.

44

Then he flung outward, feet first, with a swish,
Kicking his way down through the air to the ground.
So was I once myself a swinger of birches.
And so I dream of going back to be.
It's when I'm weary of considerations,
And life is too much like a pathless wood
Where your face burns and tickles with the cobwebs
Broken across it, and one eye is weeping
From a twig's having lashed across it open.
I'd like to get away from earth awhile
And then come back to it and begin over.
May no fate willfully misunderstand me
And half grant what I wish and snatch me away
Not to return. Earth's the right place for love:
I don't know where it's likely to go better.
I'd like to go by climbing a birch tree,
And climb black branches up a snow-white trunk
Toward heaven, till the tree could bear no more,
But dipped its top and set me down again.
That would be good both going and coming back.
One could do worse than be a swinger of birches.

Birches are flexible trees. You can climb up into one until it can barely support your weight, then kick out, and the tree will bow you to the ground, and then lift you up again. For Frost, that movement suggests a much larger meaning about how we are to live our lives.

MENDING WALL

Something there is that doesn't love a wall,
That sends the frozen-ground swell under it,
And spills the upper boulders in the sun;
And makes gaps even two can pass abreast.
The work of hunters is another thing:
I have come after them and made repair
Where they have left not one stone on a stone,
But they would have the rabbit out of hiding,
To please the yelping dogs. The gaps I mean,
No one has seen them made or heard them made,
But at spring mending-time we find them there.
I let my neighbor know beyond the hill;
And on a day we meet to walk the line
And set the wall between us once again.
We keep the wall between us as we go.
To each the boulders that have fallen to each.
And some are loaves and some so nearly balls
We have to use a spell to make them balance:
"Stay where you are until our backs are turned."
We wear our fingers rough with handling them.
Oh, just another kind of outdoor game,
One on a side. It comes to little more:
There where it is we do not need the wall:
He is all pine and I am apple orchard.
My apple trees will never get across
And eat the cones under his pines, I tell him.
He only says, "Good fences make good neighbors."
Spring is the mischief in me, and I wonder
If I could put a notion in his head:
"*Why* do they make good neighbors? Isn't it
Where there are cows? But here there are no cows.
Before I built a wall I'd ask to know
What I was walling in or walling out,
And to whom I was like to give offense.
Something there is that doesn't love a wall,
That wants it down." I could say "Elves" to him,
But it's not elves exactly, and I'd rather
He said it for himself. I see him there,

Bringing a stone grasped firmly by the top
In each hand, like an old-stone savage armed.
He moves in darkness as it seems to me,
Not of woods only and the shade of trees.
He will not go behind his father's saying,
And he likes having thought of it so well
He says again, "Good fences make good neighbors."

*If you own a rock wall—and there are many of
these in New England, spread across fields to mark
the boundaries of land—each spring you need to
walk along the wall and replace the stones that the
winter ice or rabbit hunters have knocked to the
ground. But this year, while he lugs the stones, Frost
begins to wonder why he needs the fence at all. His
neighbor has a ready answer.*

Index